"....it was Sunday and it was raining and it was Oregon."

John Steinbeck
Travels With Charley

ORYGONE III

or, everything you always wanted to know about Oregon, but were afraid to find out.

James Cloutier

By James Cloutier

IMAGE WEST PRESS · EUGENE, OREGON

This book is an outgrowth of the Oregon Ungreeting Cards, a concept created and written by a good friend, Frank Beeson. I wish to thank him for letting me use some of his original lines. I also want to express my gratitude to two other friends, Ron Abell and Bob Bury for the ideas they contributed to this book.

Quote on first page from *Travels With Charley* by John Steinbeck
Copyright © 1961, 1962 by The Curtis Publishing Co., Inc.
Copyright © 1962 by John Steinbeck
Reprinted by permission of The Viking Press

GENERAL INFORMATION

The population of Oregon is 2 million umbrellas and 4 million wet feet.

The state's main industry is distilling rain water and shipping it to California in exchange for hot air.

The largest small town in Oregon is Portland, also known as "Ripped City" because so many folks there are high on basketball.

The state capital is located at Salem but it's been suggested that we move it to Boring or Windy Point over in Crook County.

The state bird is the mosquito.

The state flower is algae.

The state rock is the sponge.

The state animal is the slug.

The state colors are gray and grayer.

The state dance is the square dance. (recently adopted by the state legislature, and we thought they just liked to go round and round)

....they rust.

People in Oregon don't tan in the summertime...

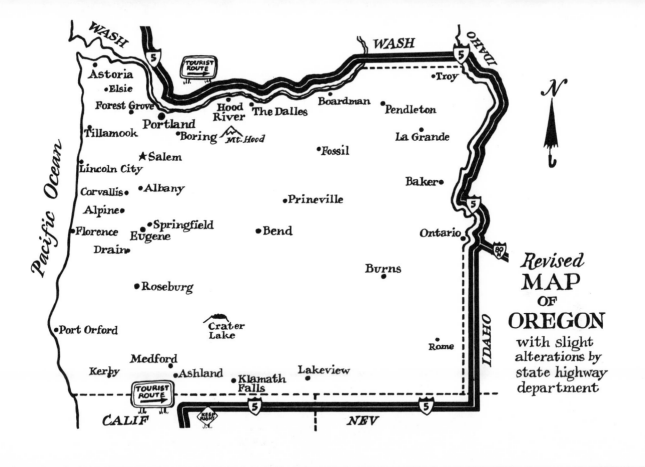

WASH

5

 TOURIST
ROUTE

Astoria
• Elsie
Forest Grove
Tillamook
Portland
• Boring
★ Salem
Lincoln City
Corvallis • • Albany
Alpine •
• Springfield
Florence • Eugene
Drain •

Hood
River • The Dalles
Mt. Hood

WASH

IDAHO

5

• Troy
Boardman
• Pendleton
La Grande

• Fossil

Baker •

Prineville

• Bend

Ontario

5

89

Burns

Rome

IDAHO

Pacific Ocean

• Roseburg

• Port Orford

Crater
Lake

Kerby Medford
• Ashland
Klamath
Falls

Lakeview

Revised
MAP
OF
OREGON
with slight
alterations by
state highway
department

TOURIST
ROUTE

CALIF

KEEP
RIGHT

5

NEV

5

N

...Idaho, Washington, Wyoming, Utah, Arizona, California, Hawaii or Afghanistan.

You'll find
Oregonians
friendly...

....when you
meet them
vacationing in
West Yellowstone.

If you can't
see Mt. Hood,
it's raining...

...if you can
see Mt. Hood,
it's just about
to rain.

In Oregon the only thing that keeps coming down while prices go up is the rain...

...and even that
soaks you.

You can tell
when summer
is near in
Oregon....

...the rain
feels warmer.

Portland ranks
among the most
beautiful cities
in the world...

... 2,954th (right
behind Calcutta)

If you're in
Salem, be sure
to visit
the state
legislature...

...it's where
somebody gets
up to say nothing,
nobody listens and
then everybody
disagrees.

Oregon's bottle bill works great....

...all we need
now is a deposit
on tourists.

We had a
mild winter
in Oregon
last year....

...but that's understandable. It came in July.

Pollution in
Albany is
getting worse...

...last week I
stopped there
to put air in my
tires and two
of them died.

Floods in Oregon
don't bother us...

...it's just
the embarassing
ring they leave
behind.

They recently painted a white line down the center of *Oregon's* Interstate 5...

...of course,
they had to
widen the road
to do it.

Corvallis,
home of the
Oregon State
Beavers...

....where the
big entertainment
on Saturday night
is going downtown
to watch haircuts.

Oregon has
a lot of
outlying
communities...

*...we can
outlie anybody.*

...they're going
to pave the
Willamette Valley.

Oregonians
never water
their lawns...

...they simply
drain them.

... probably because
so many husbands
are out for several
nights running.

For a city of its size, Springfield certainly has a lot of culture...

....unfortunately,
it's all in the
yogurt factory.

Last year in Oregon 677 people fell off their bikes...

...and drowned.

It will be safe
to visit Oregon
this summer...

...we hired a
Dutch kid to
keep his finger
in the dike.

In the town of Drain everyone looks forward to election day....

...they always hope for a big run-off.

The rain in Oregon makes everything so green....

...especially
the poison oak.

The motels
in Roseburg
finally have
hot and cold
running water...

....hot in the summer and cold in the winter.

You can always tell an Oregon native.....

...by the moss
growing on the
north side of
his nose.

In Oregon there are several resorts that overlook beautiful lakes...

...they also overlook
good food and
comfortable beds.

There are three
great things
about Medford...

...if you know
what they are,
please write the
Medford Chamber
of Commerce.

Last year in Oregon we had a total eclipse of the sun...

... too bad no
one saw it.

This year in
Oregon we have
a water shortage...

...it's only up
to our ankles
instead of our
knees.

Residents of Ashland are proud of their Shakespearean Festival.....

...of course, most
of them still think
that Hamlet is
a place with a
tavern and two
filling stations.

We were going to build a wall around the state of Oregon....

...but with our
luck it would
become a tourist
attraction.

Port Orford is a quiet Oregon coastal town...

...in fact, it's
so dull the tide
went out one
day and never
came back.

We don't worry about fashions in Oregon...

...if you've
seen one wetsuit,
you've seen
them all.

You can tell
a sunlamp
made in Oregon...

....when you
turn it on, it
  drizzles.

Residents along the Oregon Coast watch the Pacific Ocean a lot.....

....they have
to. It comes
through town
twice a day.

Oregonians
love the roar of
an approaching
storm....

....there's nothing like the sound of 2,000,000 opening umbrellas.

We wanted to bring you a few words from one of Oregon's healthiest, happiest residents...

...but we didn't
know how to
interview a
mushroom.

The Oregon Coast is truly a wonderland...

...you wonder
when it's going
to stop raining.

Whatever you want, Lincoln City's 13 Miracle Miles has it....

...and whatever
you don't want,
there's plenty
of that, too.

The speed in Oregon is 55 knots per hour...

...with no passing
on waterfalls.

...but nobody
knew it. The
pot holes in
the road took
up all the slack.

You can tell
when it's spring
in Astoria...

....the fog
gets greener.

People in Oregon
love to see
out-of-staters...

...send us some
photographs of
yourself when
you get the chance.

Visit wild, exciting, fun-filled Forest Grove...

...it's where old
folks go to visit
their grandparents.
(and if you don't like
 Forest Grove, try Newberg)

Driving on Portland's 82nd avenue is like eating an artichoke....

...you have
to go through
so much to
find so little.

One of Oregon's utilities has started drilling for geothermal energy....

...which just goes
to show you...they
don't know their
gas from a hole
in the ground.

Visitors to Oregon
marvel at the
indescribable
beauty of the
Columbia River
Gorge.....

...otherwise
known as The
Great Windtunnel
of the Northwest.

In Oregon
the rain falls
on the just and
the unjust....

...but mostly on
the just because
their umbrellas
were ripped off
by the unjust.

The Hood
River Valley is
a beautiful
place to live...

....if you
happen to be
an apple.

Last year in Oregon.....

....summer fell
on a Sunday
and more people
got to enjoy it.
(except those who
slept in)

The city of
Prineville is so
small they don't
even have a
town drunk....

...so everyone
takes a turn.

The water in
Central Oregon
is all pasturized...

...it runs through
pasture after
pasture after
pasture.

Fly fishing around Bend is fantastic....

...especially in
the Deschutes,
the great carp
stream of America.

There's a beautiful resort lodge in Central Oregon where people go for a change and rest...

...the maids get
the change and
the lodge gets
the rest.

Last year in Oregon only 20% of the population caught colds...

...the other 80% came down with pneumonia.

If you want to look at pelicans, drive to Klamath Falls....

...it's for the birds.

You'll enjoy the scenic drive between Lakeview and Ontario...

....it's miles
and miles of
miles and miles.

A drought
in Oregon...

...is a clear
day. (usually
July 26th or so)

Plan to visit Burns, the thriving metropolis of Eastern Oregon...

...where the
all-night bowling
alley closes at
4 in the afternoon.

People in Oregon
don't take showers...

...they just dry off.

The weather in Baker is very unpredictable. One day last summer they had...

...thundershowers
accompanied by
dust storms followed
by intermittent
mud flurries.

Shopping in
LaGrande is
certainly
exciting...

....it's where
grocery stores
stock cottage
cheese in the
gourmet section.

One winter
in Oregon
it snowed
and covered
all the rain...

...the following summer it rained and melted all the snow.

See Eastern Oregon, the great high country... ..where the old West still lives.

....rattlesnake
season opens May 1
and lasts through
November.

You'll get a big kick out of the famous Pendleton Roundup....

...where it's a relief to see the bull throw people for a change.

In beautiful downtown Boardman, you can now park as long as you want to...

....but you probably won't want to.

In The Dalles you can play blackjack and bingo but not the slot machine...

....they have a
law banning the
use of a steel
trap for catching
dumb animals.

In Oregon
we have rain
for breakfast,
rain for lunch,
rain for dinner...

.....and when it doesn't rain we starve to death. (the last case of starvation was on July 26, 1902 in Fossil, Oregon)

...convertible owners have been driving around with their tops down for years.

Only in Oregon did Humpty Dumpty have a bad fall...

...and a lousy
summer and
a wet spring
and a terrible
winter.

Salem... site of the state capital, state penitentiary and state mental hospital....

...only one of
the preceding is
is run by its
inmates.

Oregonians
recently sighted
a U.F.O.....

....the Sun.

Oregonians
know how to
do a rain
dance.....

...it's called
"crossing the
street."

The city of Eugene, Oregon leads the nation......

...in fallen arches,
jock itch and
athlete's foot.
(not to mention hay
fever, poison oak and
tooth decay)

For information about the state of Oregon, write the Chamber of Commerce....

...which is closed
due to a lack of
information and
commerce.

ABOUT THE AUTHOR

James Cloutier is an eclectic artist and native Oregonian whose great grandparents homesteaded in Wallowa County near Troy in 1892. He presently resides in Eugene with his six cats and is currently working on a third book *An Oregon Sketchbook*. His first book, recently published, is titled *ALPINE, OREGON, Photographs of a Small Town in America*. Its text and finely reproduced black and white photographs focus on the town's tavern as a social gathering place.

STATE OF OREGON (ORYGONE)
PASSPORT AND VISA APPLICATION

PHOTOGRAPH (Not Mandatory) We don't care what you look like as long as you look like you're not going to stay.	TO BE COMPLETED BY ALL APPLICANTS PLANNING TO VISIT OREGON (Please print or type)
	(FIRST NAME) **(MIDDLE NAME)** **(LAST NAME)**
	MAIL PASSPORT TO: STREET_____ CITY_____ STATE_____ ZIP CODE_____

SEX (Yes or No)	HEIGHT (Enough to keep head above water)	COLOR OF HAIR (If bald, leave blank)	COLOR OF EYES (Red not acceptable)	BIRTHPLACE (If California, lie)

Answer with Yes or No	CAN YOU SWIM?	IF NO, CAN YOU FLOAT?	DOES YOUR CAR FLOAT?	DOES YOUR CAR HAVE 4 WHEEL DRIVE?	OUTBOARD MOTOR?	SURVIVAL KIT?

DO YOU OWN AN UMBRELLA?	IF YES, HOW MANY? IF NO, BUY SEVERAL	DO YOU OWN A LIFE JACKET?	IF YES, HOW MANY IF NO, BORROW ONE	DO YOU SUFFER FROM ANY OF THE FOLLOWING CONDITIONS: WATER-ON-THE-KNEE, FOOT FUNGUS OR POST-NASAL DRIP?

IF NO, GET APPROPRIATE VACCINATIONS IF YES, CONSIDER VACATION IN CARACAS	DO YOU RUST EASILY? IF YES, BRING NAVAL JELLY	DO YOU ENJOY CHANGING FLAT TIRES IN SIX INCHES OF MUDDY WATER? (John Steinbeck didn't)	DOES THE CONSTANT SOUND OF DRIP, DRIP, DRIP KEEP YOU AWAKE? ...WHILE DRIVING?

OCCUPATION (If a realtor or land developer, stay home and we'll send you post cards)	REASON FOR VISITING OREGON? (We'll provide the reason for leaving)

I hereby solemnly swear that the statements made on this page are not all wet.

_____   _____

Day   Month   Year   Signature of applicant

INFORMATION FOR PASSPORT APPLICANTS

A. WHO MAY BE ISSUED A PASSPORT

1. Anyone, but preference given to prospective visitors planning a 24 hour vacation to Oregon.

2. Families may apply for a single passport.

B. USE OF THIS FORM

1. In filling out, only name and address are mandatory. Other questions are relevant but optional.

2. Unless specifically limited by the Governor of Oregon to a shorter period of validity, passports are valid for a period of forty (40) days and forty (40) nights from date of entry. Then the Ark sails.

C. VISA INFORMATION

1. Included in passport is a visa good for one temporary, limited, non-residential visit to Oregon. Visa is valid for thirty (30) days as long as bearer keeps moving. Thoughts of settling down are grounds for immediate revocation.

D. PASSPORT FEES

1. Amount of Fee. The fee for a passport and visa is $2.

2. Form of Fee. The following forms of remittance are acceptable:
   a. Cash - for keeping Oregon green
   b. Check - any kind on paper
   c. Money Order

E. IMMUNIZATION INFORMATION

1. Under the International Health Regulations adopted by the World Health Organization, an International Certificate of Vaccination against meandering mildew of the mind may be required as a condition of entry to Oregon. On the other hand, you could always take your chances with this affliction more commonly known in Oregon as water-on-the-brain.

This application should be filled out and returned with passport fee to: Oregon Passport Agency, % Image West Press, Box 5511, Eugene, Oregon 97405.